ISBN-13: 978-1523907625

Disclaimer

Cover design: Cherie Johnsonⓦ

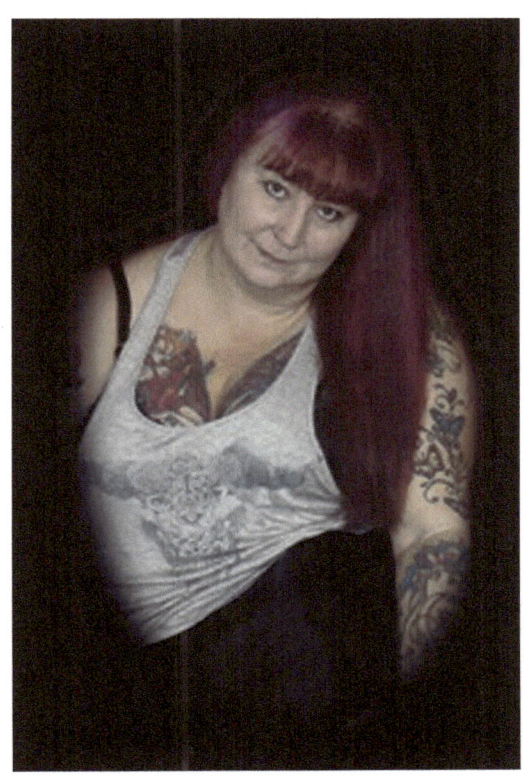

About the Author

Cherie Johnson is from Alberta, Canada. She received her diploma in Visual Communications in 1991 and worked in advertising design and instruction for 10 years. Cherie has been tattooing since 2002. Cherie has owned and operated her own tattoo shop where she works as a tattoo artist since 2004 and has done over 6500 tattoos in her career so far.

Dedication

This book is dedicated to my Mom Joyce and my wonderful Husband Don, who both support me whole heartedly in every endeavour I undertake. Without their love and support I would never have accomplished all that I have in my life!

Index

Introduction

Unless you have spent most of your recent time in a cave or a monastery you can hardly have failed to notice the growing number of adults sporting "epidermal artwork", be it a postage-stamp sized flower or a dragon covering three-quarters of someone's body. Tats, ink, body art or just plain tattoos, they seem to be everywhere, and if you do not have one yet you know a lot of people who do. It wouldn't be surprising should you, like many of the "un-inked" people out there, have at least once considered joining the colored crowd.

Perhaps you're nervous and don't have a clue where to start. This is understandable because getting a tattoo is a life changing event, whether it is your first tattoo or your 21st tattoo. Having a tattoo permanently inked on your body is a very personal and in many cases, healing experience. Trying to decide on a tattoo, what to get, where to get it, what artists to get to do it for you, can be a daunting task, because lets face it, it's permanent!

As a tattoo professional I am often asked questions by the timid, the nervous and the just plain curious. Getting a bit tired of answering the same questions over and over, I finally decided to sit down and grab the monkey by the balls, answer all the 7

questions in one easy to read book and hopefully help you out.

I have tried to deal with the following issues surrounding

getting inked as simply as possible; I sincerely hope that you find it at least a little bit helpful when you make the necessary decisions.

How to plan your tattoo, what will work as a tattoo and what will not work.

How to find the best shop and artist for your tattoo.

How tattoos are priced and how much your tattoo will cost you.

Learn the many things about you and your skin that will effect the tattoo.

You will find out what will happen the day of your tattoo so you can be prepared and how to look after your new tattoo afterwards.

You will even learn the process of how a tattoo is applied.

In our business we do at least 2 cover ups or tattoo rescues a week and often many more than that. There are a lot of people that have tattoos they are not happy with, this book is designed to help you avoid being one of these people. Think Before You're Inked covers everything you need to know about the tattoo journey from beginning to the end, so you can be safe and get the best tattoo possible.

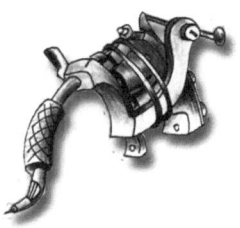

Chapter 1

Why Get tattooed?

There are many life changing events that happen in your life however a tattoo is one of only a handful that will be with you forever. Lasting well beyond any other purchase you will ever make for yourself, and something that you will take to the grave with you.

Body art is permanent marker in your life, a personal experience you won't ever forget. A person can look at every tattoo they have and remember often down to the day and hour when they got it, what the weather was like, how they were feeling, who was with them and where they were. The feeling you have when you get your tattoo be it joy, pain, sadness, stubbornness, rebellion, whatever the feeling, those feelings will be indelibly inked into your skin.

There are so many different reasons you may be getting your tattoo it could be to represent joy or love, healing, change, triumph, just for fun or even anger. These emotions will be re-experienced each time you look at the tattoo. Also the very nature of having a tattoo applied to your body lends it self exceptionally well to emotional, spiritual, mental and even physical healing.

Without even being aware of the nuances of receiving a tattoo many people choose to get tattooed as a way of healing a painful past. A tattoo in this case being representative of triumph over a painful physical, emotional or mental incident in their life. This could be a mentally painful past, a physically painful trauma, the passing of a loved one, or anything else that has left a painful scar either mentally, emotionally or physically on the body that the person wants to move past and heal.

There are studies that show getting tattoos are good for you. Besides the obvious outlet of self expression, these studies have proven that getting inked is good for you. Not only can a tattoo boost your body image, they are also a beautiful way to hide scars and marks that are causing you unwanted distress.

The pain involved in getting a tattoo causes your body to release adrenalin and this makes you feel very much alive. This adrenalin rush can make almost anyone feel amazing especially the adrenalin junkie. Not only that, you also experience a rush of endorphins, these are chemicals that are produced to make us feel good. Endorphins are your bodies natural pain relief system. So while you are trying to cope with the pain of getting a tattoo, your brain is helping you out by releasing pain blocking chemicals, these in turn can make you feel good. Then there is the fact that the pain receptors in your brain are associated closely with the pleasure receptors and when you are in pain such as when you get tattooed some of these receptors get crossed and this can make your pain feel rewarding. You still feel the pain however it becomes associated with pleasure which will make you think getting a tattoo feels good.

Although becoming more popular and accepted in society today, tattoos have a sordid past. Many people still look 'down their nose' at body art. It can be a daunting task to change the way some have been taught to think about certain things including body art. In many cases it may be those closest to you that are opposed to you getting tattooed.

On the bright side the way body art is viewed has slowly changed over the last century and it has become much more acceptable to have a visible tattoo. No longer are tattoos only for criminals and rebels, they are becoming an acceptable form of self expression among all levels of society. This change in perception was definitely helped by the advent of reality television shows depicting body art in a positive light. Showing everyday people, among them grandparents, doctors, policeman, soccer moms, judges, CEO's and others getting meaningful tattoos, and has done amazing things in changing how society views body art. These shows fast tracked the change in the mindset of people on how they view tattoos, if that policeman, doctor, grandma or soccer mom, can get a tattoo and it is okay, then I can get one too.

Body art sets itself apart as a luxury purchase, it is a purchase that often people have to 'save up' for, and because of this a lot of thought is put into getting a tattoo, not only that it is permanent. Tattoos are not like a new hair color or cut which will eventually grow out and can be changed fairly easily if you don't like it. Once a tattoo is done it is staying exactly where it is, as it is, not going anywhere without great effort and cost.

Whether it is your first tattoo, your first tattoo in a 'real shop' or one among many, there are a lot of decisions to be made.

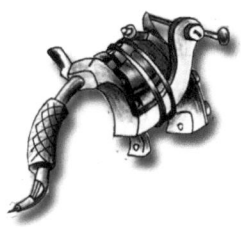

Chapter 2

How A Tattoo Is Done

A tattoo is done by a group of very fine needles which can be in a round grouping or in a grouping that looks like a flat paintbrush is inserted into a tube that goes into the tattoo machine which drives the needles very fast up and down in the tube. The needles and tube together look like a pen, the needles only extending out of the tube a tiny bit. Most likely you will not even be able to see the needles at all if you were to watch the process being done. The needles are dipped into the tattoo pigment and then they are placed against the skin like drawing with a pen and the needles inject the color into the skin. The color is injected to a fraction of an inch. Skin is very thin if you think about your skin peeling when you have a sunburn that is how thin the top layer of skin is. The ink from a tattoo is only injected just below your epidermis the top layers of your skin and the epidermis is only .06 - .20 mm thick to the deepest layer of your epidermis. So a tattoo does not go deeper than an 1/8 or an inch into your skin.

The layer of skin your tattoo ends up resting against is a

single layer of cells which rests on a membrane that separates the top layer of your skin from the bottom layer of skin, the dermis. This membrane is called the papillary. The papillary layer contains finger like projections that can contain capillaries which are tiny veins, and corpuscles which are sensory touch receptors or nerves.

As your tattoo heals your top layer of skin called Keratin will peel off like a sunburn and regenerate thus sealing your tattoo into your skin.

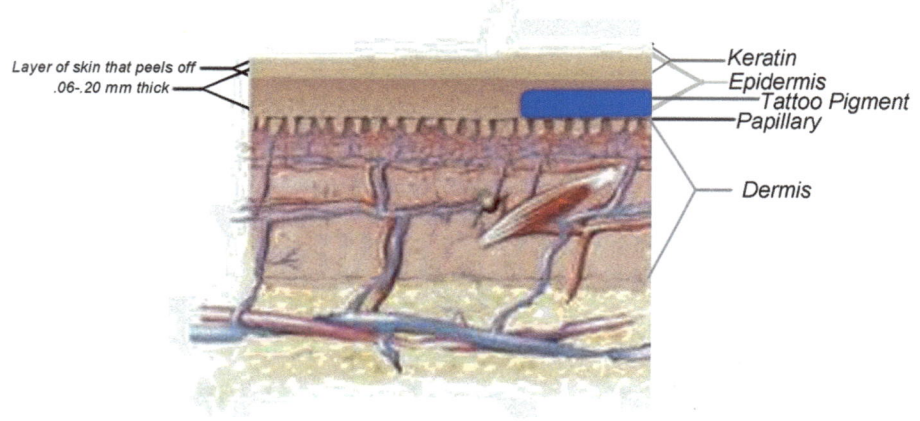

If a tattoo is not properly done the ink can be injected beyond the papillary layer of skin, the layer that separates the first layer of skin from the second layer of skin, and end up in the dermis the fatty thicker layer of skin. As a result of the ink being injected too deep, the dermis acts like a sponge and the tattoo ink will spread out from the area of the original tattoo causing your tattoo to look fuzzy on the edges. When this happens it is in the tattoo industry called a blow out. When tattoo pigment is injected too deep it can also cause scarring in the area of your tattoo. Scarring causes your tattoo to have raised areas that can sometimes be itchy. Sometimes with minor scarring your tattoo may only feel raised and slightly irritated or itchy when it is hot or it has been exposed to the sun. If the tattoo pigment is injected too shallow into only the top layer of skin, then most of the color will peel away as the skin heals and you will be left with a very faded old looking tattoo or in the worst case no tattoo at all.

The more experience and thus the more practice a tattoo artist has the more they will know about how to work with different types of skin and the better they will be at doing a tattoo that will heal quickly and well.

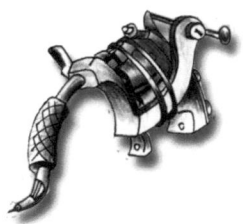

Chapter 3

Deciding On A Tattoo Design

Some people know exactly what they want to get tattooed others know they want a tattoo but not what to get. If you are unsure what to get you can start by making a list of what is important to you, what you are proud of, what makes you happy every time you look at it or think of it. Perhaps you love working on vehicles and rebuilt a classic car this would be great subject matter for a tattoo. If you are a proud parent you can plan a tattoo that represents your children. Perhaps you feel happy every time you see honey bees or roses, do rainy spring days have happy memories? A hobby you love might make a great tattoo, it could be anything from cooking to hunting, mud bogging, gardening, sewing, etc. Perhaps you have lost something or someone you love. Memorial tattoos are used as a way to carry something you loved and have lost with you forever. Maybe you have overcome an obstacle in your life you could plan a tattoo in celebration of that.

There are no silly ideas for tattoos, if it means something

or is important to you that is where you start. Looking up the symbolism of different images can help you decide what to incorporate into your new tattoo as well.

Tattoo Ideas Brainstorming Page

Things I Love	Things I Am Proud Of	Things That Make Me Happy	Hobbies

Once you have an idea that appeals to you the internet is a great way to get ideas on what you would like your tattoo to look like. Be sure to keep in mind that just because the tattoo or artwork you are looking at fits on the screen of your smart phone does not mean it is or can be done at that size. The more small detail you want to have in your tattoo the larger it is going to have to be to age well and look good over time, and really you want a tattoo that is going to look great the day you get it AND in 20, 30 and even 40 years. If your getting your ideas from the internet and are unsure what size a tattoo is from looking at the pictures you find, be prepared for your tattoo artist to let you know that what you thought would be $120 tattoo is in actuality a $600 tattoo and needs to be simplified if you would like it a smaller size.

One way to get an idea if a tattoo can be done as small as you would like it and you have access to a printer and a program to print your images the size you want, is to find a picture you like then print it the size you would like it to be. Get yourself a fine tip sharpie marker and then trace over all the lines on the image the size you think you would like it. If the lines bleed together and the image starts looking like a blob then the design you picked at the size you printed off will most likely not work as a tattoo at the size you want it to be.

When planning your tattoo keep in mind that straight lines and circles are very hard to keep consistent and perfect, the larger they are the harder it will be. Your body is not flat so straight lines and perfect circles tend to distort on the curved surfaces of the body. Words are very popular and can be beautiful however keep in mind that words, especially done in script are very hard to do perfectly and the smaller you want your script to be the less consistent it will be. Writing will never look the same on your skin tattooed as it does when printed out on a piece of paper from a computer. Tattoo artists are not machines and your skin is a living moving thing not a flat piece of paper. If your thinking of getting a meaningful quote keep in mind the longer the quote the more space it is going to need on your body.

Ink spreads under the skin over time as your skin changes and you age so very small close together detail on a tattoo including writing will not age well, as over time the lines will spread slightly, often making a tattoo that looked great fresh unreadable over time. You can use the fine tip sharpie marker trick to trace over the tattoo you want and see what happens especially to small spaces like the space inside of letters like the e's. In the case of writing the larger you can get it the better it will age and look over time.

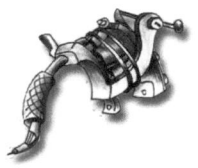

Deciding where to put your tattoo

Location, location, location.....

When trying to decide where to put your tattoo there are a few things you will want to keep in mind. First do you want to be able to see it or is it just for other people to enjoy. You will not be able to see tattoos on your back well and as a result you may tend to forget you even have them, as this is an area you can only see on yourself when you make a special effort to look at it in the mirror. Also little tattoos behind your ears can often become out of sight out of mind tattoos over time.

If your tattoo is a representation of a living or mythical being such as a person, animal, dragon etc. it is understood among the tattoo industry that these should always be facing forward looking towards the future not face backwards looking at the past.

When placing your tattoos on your lower arms or wrists think about whether you want it placed facing yourself or facing others. Keep in mind that if you decide to have your tattoo facing you, to everyone else who looks at it your tattoo will be upside down. If you can not decide another idea for placement is sideways on your arm or wrist so when you raise your arm to look at it is right side up however when your arm is relaxed it is sideways not upside down.

Getting your tattoo on your arms or legs are great options when you want to be able to see and enjoy your tattoo. Placement on a chest is also a good spot if you want to be able to see your tattoo but keep it hidden.

If you want to be able to keep your tattoo covered a tattoo can be placed on the upper part of your arms as most T-shirts will cover this area, any part of your legs especially the upper part if you wear skirts or shorts to work and on your back and chest are relatively easy to keep covered up if this is a priority for you.

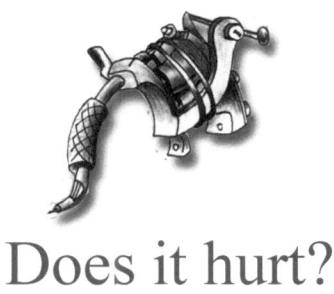

Chapter 4

Does it hurt?

Every person has a different tolerance for pain and each person can also have different levels of tolerance to pain on different days. If you are sick, already in pain for some reason or just having a bad day emotionally this can lower your pain tolerance.

Every part of your body can feel different moreover you can experience several different feelings while getting a single tattoo, pain, itchiness, ticklishness, or even pleasure, yes pleasure.

Every person feels pain differently as well so describing how it feels to someone else is very difficult. The feeling of getting a tattoo is a unique feeling and until you have experienced getting a tattoo it will be difficult to understand what it feels like. Some of the ways tattoo pain has been described are, a cat scratch on a sun burn, something hot dragging on the skin or like an electric shock. Many people actually enjoy getting tattooed and find the sensation pleasant.

Generally there are areas of your body that hurt more or

less than others. Here are some general rules of to keep in mind when picking a spot to tattoo:

- -Less fat between the area of your skin that is getting tattooed and the bones underneath is going to cause your tattoos to be more painful. Places like the top of head, elbows, knees, ankles , etc.

- -Areas of skin that are not always covered or protected and exposed to the sun and elements will be less painful. Places like the outer arms, some parts of your legs and necks.

- -Your nerves are more concentrated as a group running from the bottom of the back of your skull from your neck to the base of your spine and down the back of your arms and legs, as a result pain receptors are more concentrated in these areas which can make a tattoo more painful.

Areas and degree of pain

Scale 1 - 10 with 1 being least and 10 being most painful:

-Top of the head ....8 -10	-Stomach............................ 6 - 9
-Neck ....3 - 5	-Back of shoulders & neck... 3 - 5
-Top of shoulders............... 5 - 7	-Middle Lower Back ....3 - 8
-Outer arms ....1 - 4	-Side & ribs ....5 - 8
-Inner arms ....4 - 7	-Breast ....2 - 4
-Wrist ....4 - 6	-Under breast ....4 - 6
-Top of hand ....2 - 4	-Buttocks ....3 - 6
-Top of fingers................... 4 - 7	-Front of Upper & lower leg .2 - 5
-Inside fingers................... 6 - 8	-Back of leg & calf ....5 - 8
-Palm of hands ....9 - 10	-Knee ....7 - 10
-Elbow ....6 - 9	-Ankle ....5 - 7
-Chest.............................. 3 - 6	-Foot..................................... 4 - 7
-Sternum...........................7 - 10	
-Armpit ....8 - 10	

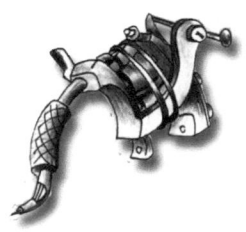

Chapter 5

Your Skin the Living Canvas

There are many factors that will determine how easy it is for your artist to do your tattoo thus how long it will take them to complete it.

If you look at your skin under a microscope you will see that your skin is like a mountain range, all peaks and valleys. Your skin is not smooth like a piece of paper therefore it is impossible for a tattoo line to be as smooth and straight as a line drawn on a piece of paper. Take a piece of paper and crumple it up and then smooth it out and try to get a perfect line on it, chances are you won't be able too.

Another thing that will effect the tattoo process is the fact your skin swells up as it gets tattooed. The more it swells the tougher it is to tattoo. The less swollen your skin is the softer it is, swelling hardens the skin making it more difficult for the tattoo needle to penetrate to the proper depth.

Goose bumps also interfere with the tattooing process.

Tattoos can be done over scarring however scarring changes the skins constancy. Light scarring is easier to tattoo than heavy scarring. The smoother and lighter your scarring the easier it will be to tattoo. Heavier scarring is harder to tattoo and there is the possibility of the tattoo over areas of scarring to heal lighter than the tattoo over your unscarred skin. The more heavily scarred your skin is the thicker and more rubbery it will be making it harder for the tattoo needles to penetrate. If you want to get a tattoo over any scarring you may have it is a good idea to give your scars at least a year to heal. The older the scars are the smoother and easier to tattoo they will be. Also if you try tattooing over a scar that is too fresh it will be much more painful.

It is possible to tattoo over stretch marks, although it is a little more difficult. There is the possibility that the tattoo will heal inconstantly in these areas thus requiring two or more tattoo sessions to make the overall tattoo color look smooth and consistent.

An artist really should not be tattooing over any moles you may have, as this could prevent you or your doctor from noticing any changes in them that could be detrimental to your health. So trying to avoid placing tattoos around any moles you have is a good idea. If you cannot avoid it you should make sure the artist is not tattooing over top of them but instead around them. If a doctor does have to remove a mole and it is in your tattoo the look of your tattoo is probably going to be affected as well.

Skin changes as it ages. The older you get the thinner your skin can get. Very young skin can be very 'tight', the pours very close together, and this can make it harder to the needle to penetrate the skin. As you age skin gets thinner and this has to be taken into consideration because the thinner the skin the easier it is to go too deep and as a result get 'blow outs' or in layman's terms fuzzy lines because the ink spreads our under the skin on either side of the tattoo lines so extra time and care has to be taken in the tattooing process.

Sun exposure also effects how easy or hard it will be for the artist to do your tattoo. We all love to spend time in the sun, when you spend time in the sun with your skin uncovered this changes your skin and can actually make it easier to tattoo. Over time, exposure to sun rays makes the skin less elastic, less elastic skin is easier to tattoo and this is a good thing. Sun exposure also helps to desensitize the skin a bit so tattoos tend to be a bit less painful. This is why arms and legs can be the easiest, fastest and least painful area for an artist to tattoo. However if you are from a hot climate and your skin is constantly exposed to the sun you skin may eventually become thickened and leathery, wrinkled, or in some cases over time thin like tissue paper and this makes it harder for a tattoo artist to tattoo.

Areas of your body that never see the sun are more elastic and this makes it more difficult to tattoo because it is harder for an artist to stretch the skin tight enough and as a result the skin acts like an elastic and the needle will bounce off the skin instead of penetrate the skin in a clean and even manner. Which is also the case if the skin being tattooed is loose making it more difficult for the artist to stretch tight.

Tattoos done on areas of your body with thinner skin can often, even when an artist takes great care, 'bleed' color out into the surrounding skin causing what looks like a shadow or bruising around your tattoo. In the case of thin skin it is more challenging for the artist to gauge the proper depth for the tattoo.

Every persons skin is unique and every area on each person has different degrees of difficulty to tattoo.

How healthy you are will be a determining factor on how well your skin will take ink. Your health will also factor into how painful your tattoo is for you on any given day. If you are sick, have the flu, fighting a cold or even generally just run down this can change the nature of your skin making it more sensitive for you and harder for the artist to tattoo. If you are on medication this also can cause the skin to be harder to tattoo.

If you have very sensitive skin or allergies and you are concerned about having an allergic reaction to the tattoo pigment most shops, for a set up fee, will tattoo a tiny test area. This way you can see if your going to react to the pigments before you get a larger tattoo. Although having a reaction to certain pigments is rare it does on occasion happen. It is not common and if your really worried black is the most unlikely pigment to cause any adverse affects when it is tattooed into your skin. The most common colors that can cause an allergic reaction are reds and greens. It is even more rare for someone to have a reaction to other colors, however you are introducing a foreign substance into your body and there is always the possibility and risk your body could try and reject it. If your skin is very swollen and itchy long after the tattoo should be or has healed chances are your body had taken a disliking to one or more of the pigments that were used in the tattoo and is trying to get rid of it. You can purchase over the counter topical cortisone creams from the pharmacy and try using them on your tattoo. If the swelling and itching does not dissipate of the next couple weeks you may need to see the doctor and get a cream with a higher dose of cortisone in it. Used as directed this should take the swelling and itching away in a few weeks.

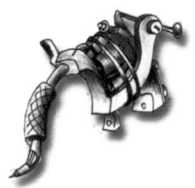

Asses, Necks, Hands, Fingers and Feet

All of these areas are all more difficult to tattoo and will take longer and not heal as well as other areas on the body.

Asses have very stretchy skin, you may think you have a tight ass but think about it, this skin has to be the stretchiest skin on your body. It also has extra fat in it to add comfort when you sit on it. The constant sitting on it in turn toughens it up. Then throw in the fact that it most likely rarely if ever sees the sun which keeps it sensitive as the nerves have not been exposed to the elements which would cause them to be less sensitive. So not only is it stretchy and tough it can be very sensitive too. So be prepared for your tattoo artist to try and talk you out of this location or even out right refuse to tattoo it at all.

Necks are one of the hardest areas to tattoo. This is another area where the skin is super stretchy and tough. Your neck is always moving and is constantly exposed to the elements. As a result of the stretchiness of the skin the ink in your neck tattoo may 'break apart' causing exposed skin lines to run through the color during the healing process. This is a result of the natural stretching of the skin on the neck which pulls the skin tighter than the artist was able to stretch it when the tattoo was done. This can result in the color 'pulling' apart as it heals. The neck is also hard to tattoo because it is awkward for an artist to tattoo, I have yet to meet an artist that enjoys tattooing a neck especially the front of a neck over a throat. Not only this, many artists will refuse to tattoo it because you cannot cover up and hide a tattoo on your neck and the artist may not want to be the one responsible for you not being able to get that future job. Like it or not some people still judge others on their exposed tattoos especially on necks and hands.

Hands and fingers are the skin on your body that takes the most abuse. They are constantly brushing up against things and exposed to the elements, they also spend the most amount of time in water. Not only that hands especially palms and fingers are very sensitive. There is also several different types of skin in a very small area. The tops of your hands are the easiest to tattoo as this skin is the best thickness and consistency to tattoo and will heal the most evenly. Fingers are much more difficult because the skin is looser and tougher especially around the joints so tattoos on the fingers tend not to heal well at all with much of the ink disappearing as it comes off with the healing skin. It is very very difficult for an artist to gauge how deep they are going on fingers. The knuckles themselves can have several different thicknesses of skin on them so this makes it impossible to tattoo to a consistent depth no matter how good your tattoo artist is. The sides of your fingers have very thin skin and on top of that are constantly rubbing together thus the skin is being shed at a faster rate. This also makes for very inconsistent healing. The palms of your hands and under your fingers are the hardest skin to tattoo and heal on your entire body. The skin is thick and regenerates very quickly and is the toughest skin on the body aside from the bottom of your feet. Palm tattoos NEVER heal solid, most of them disappearing within weeks of having them done. This is because of the thickness of this particular skin an artist simply can not tattoo to the proper depth. Again do not be surprised that a large percentage of tattoo artists will refuse to tattoo hands especially the insides and under fingers and the palms. These tattoos are not only very difficult to do they notoriously heal terrible and look bad once they are healed, and many artist do not want there skill level judged on tattoos they know are going to heal badly. Remember it is hard to judge how badly these tattoos heal by looking at pictures of them on the internet. Most pictures of tattoos posted on the internet are of fresh tattoos right after they are done not pictures of them healed. Fresh tattoos can very often look way better than they do healed.

Foot tattoos can easily become inflamed and/or infected. They are the closest to the ground and thus it is easy for contaminants to be introduced into the tattoo causing complications in healing like infections. The skin on the top of the foot tends to be thinner making it harder for an artist to tattoo. If you are going to get a foot tattoo it is important to find an artist who has experience tattooing feet. Extra care and attention must be taken in the healing of this area as well.

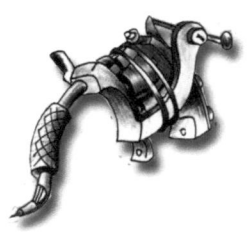

Chapter 6

Finding An Artist
Getting your artwork done & \|
booking an appointment

The harsh reality now a days is that not all tattoo artists are created equal. So you really need to do your due diligence when looking for an artist. Sure in days gone by there were always people experimenting with homemade tattoo guns, sewing needles and indian ink, who proceeded to give out bad tattoos. However with the ready availability of professional tattoo supplies on the internet it is very easy for anyone to purchase what they need and start tattooing, either in their home or even sometimes in a shop, with no experience, training or mentorship. So when before you knew an artist was not a professional artist because they were tattooing you with a homemade tattoo gun now the lines are not so clear as anyone can purchase professional machines, power supplies, needles, tubes and ink on the internet. Sure every artist started somewhere and if they are honest with how much experience they have and your okay going to someone with less experience that's great, however not everyone is going to be up front on how much experience and training they may have.

If you see someone with beautifully healed artwork on their bodies do not be afraid to ask them where they got it from. When you look through an artists portfolio look for pictures of healed tattoos as well as fresh because a lot of times tattoos can look fantastic fresh and when they heal they do not look the same. Most shops now have online portfolios that you can look through if you feel uncomfortable going into a lot of tattoo shops.

There are a lot of tattoo artists that specialize in different areas, when you are looking for an artist ask them what they specialize in or what they love to do, they will more likely than not be more well versed in doing this style of tattoo. When your looking through a portfolio, look at the line work on a tattoo, it should be smooth and solid as good line work, unless your going for realism, is the basis for a great tattoo.

If you do not have a tattoo artist, go to a few shops and talk to different artists, find one you feel understands and is able to do the tattoo you want. When looking for a studio, look at how clean it is. Your getting an invasive procedure done and you want it done in a clean environment. Look at the artists portfolios. Be honest with yourself when deciding if the style of work they do appeals to you. If it does give the artist your ideas and see what they have to say. If you don't like what your hearing or agree with it go to another shop and ask another artist. Go to a few different shops if you are hearing different things from different artists, you may hear the same thing from a few artists such as what you want will not look good at the size you want. If you hear the same thing from several artists then that is most likely the case. If you look long and hard enough you may find that one artist that will tell you they can do it exactly like you want it done however if you have had a few artists advise against it or refuse to do it the way you envision it, it would be wise to take the advice of the many over the one who is willing to do it.

Pick an artist and a shop that you feel comfortable with. Every shop and every artist is different.

If you have access to a printer, print off all the ideas you have for your tattoo to give to your artist for reference. Bring your ideas into your artist and discuss what you would like. If you have a budget let them know what that is as well, they will be able to tell you whether or not what you want will be able to be done within that budget. Your artist will be able to take your ideas and design it just for you, to fit the area you want to fit and depending on what your idea was, revise that idea if necessary to fit within your budget.

Be open and willing to changes to your design ideas. Good tattoo artists know what looks the best as far as size, detail and arrangement to fit the part of your body you want your tattoo on. If you have looked at the artist portfolio and like what you see in it then chances are great that you will be able to come up with an idea together that will make you happy. Remember this is 'your' tattoo you are the one who will have to look at it forever so be sure you love the final concept because if you don't you could regret getting it after it is done.

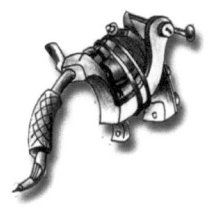

The Deposit

It is common practice for an artist to take a deposit when you decide to have them start designing your tattoo. Deposit amounts very from shop to shop. Sometimes these deposits cover the artists time to design the tattoo, and in other shops the deposit may come off the cost of the tattoo when you get it done. In many shops your deposit is not refundable.

Deposits are often required to guarantee your appointment time, if something comes up and you need to change your appointment each shop has a 'deadline' that this can be done by or you lose your deposit. In many shops this is around 2 or 3 days before the appointment. If you 'miss' your appointment and have not called to change it within the amount of time allowed you will lose your deposit. This is a practice followed by most shops because an artist can only tattoo one person at a time and they do not get paid if they are not tattooing, tattooing is not a job you get paid an hourly wage for whether you are working or not. So if a client for whatever reason just does not show up on the day of their appointment, the tattoo artist has not had any time to book another client into that spot so they spend that time not tattooing and not getting paid.

If you are wanting something small and relatively easy some shops will tattoo the day you come in as a walk in. Sometimes shops have one day of the week were they only do walk in appointments.

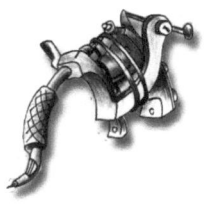

Cost

The cost of a tattoo will depend on how big a tattoo is and how much detail it has. Know what you want before you ask how much it is going to cost. When the artist asks 'What do you want?' at least have a good idea in mind of what you would like, how big you want it and where you want to put it. The best an artist can do is give you is a general idea of what a tattoo will cost until they know exactly what you want and what size you want it. If your not sure what you want think of someone else's tattoo you liked and ask how much a similar tattoo in size and detail would be. You could also ask what the shops minimum charge is and what size of a tattoo that would be. Ask your friends that live in the same area as you how much their tattoos cost.

If you have a budget, be realistic and aware of what shops are charging for tattoos in your area because if you have a $50 budget in mind when the minimum charge in most shops is $100, your budget is unrealistic. When you speak with an artist let them know your budget. This will help the artist determine if you can get what you have in mind. Often if your open to changes the artist can work with you to stay within your budget and still give you something you will love even if it is not exactly the same as what you wanted to start with.

Cost can vary from shop to shop and from city to city.

The price of body art like all things is affected by supply and demand, the experience of each individual artist also factors in. Most shops have a minimum charge. This charge is a basic cost for even the smallest tattoo, this is put in place because regardless of how small a tattoo may be there is still basic costs involved including time and supplies used to do the tattoo.

For example: a tattoo the size of a quarter and a tattoo 2"x 2", will use the same amount of supplies, even thought the smaller tattoo takes less time to do. Also keep in mind that if it is a small tattoo you are getting, it is still permanent and you want the best job done on the tattoo you can get. Just because it is a tiny tattoo does not make it any easier to do in a lot of cases, being a tiny tattoo can complicate the process and make it harder for an artist to do.

There are two main ways tattoos are charged out by, one is by the piece and the other is by the hour. One reason artist charge out by the piece is because they have a lot of experience and with experience comes the ability to finish a tattoo faster than average, or on the end of the spectrum an artist may not have as much experience and they take more time to do a great job and as a result they are slower than average. Charging by the piece ensures that the tattoo is being charged at a comparable and fair rate in comparison to other shops and artists in the area.

Being charged by the hour means you pay an hourly rate for the time it takes to complete your tattoo.

So whether the artist charges by the hour or by the piece you will find if you compare tattoo size and detail to cost between artists with the same experience, most of the time they will be comparable in cost.

For example: a very experienced artist may charge by the piece and will be able to do your 3" x 3" tattoo start to finish in 45 minutes with a total cost to you of $150, and an artist in a shop down the street may charge $100 an hour take an 1 1/2 hrs to do the same tattoo to comparable standards and that tattoo will also work out to be $150. An advantage of going to a shop that charges by the piece is that if your tattoo does take longer to do than the artist estimated it would, you are not paying more for the tattoo, however if your tattoo is being charged by the hour you will pay for the time regardless how long it takes so if you were given an estimate that the tattoo will take 1 hour and it takes the artist 2 hours to complete you pay double the original estimate. This can get confusing and may often seem like you will get a better deal paying for your tattoo by the hour, however complications can come up that will bring the cost of the tattoo up.

The experience of an artist will also effect the cost, artists with more years of experience may charge more as their experience and knowledge in working with different types of skin in different conditions and locations on the body along with their experience in working with a wider genre of tattoos is worth the extra cost.

Each shop may have a different policy on how they charge out by the hour as well, for example one shop may be a flat rate hourly charge, so if your tattoo takes one hour and fifteen minutes you will be paying for two hours worth of time. Another shop may charge a pro rated fee, this would mean the first hour of time is charged out at the hourly fee and then you are charged a pro rated fee, most likely half the hourly rate charged up to each half hour spent tattooing. So if your tattoo takes an hour and fifteen minutes your are paying 1.5 times the hourly rate if your tattoo takes an hour and forty-five minutes our tattoo will be charged for 2 hours. Some shops may even break it down to 15 minute increments. Be sure to ask before you get your tattoo.

Small tattoos will usually cost you less than $250. The larger the tattoo the more you are going to have to pay. Full sleeves and back pieces are not cheap, a well planned, well done sleeve or back piece can cost you thousands of dollars as they take dozens of hours to complete.

As tattoos are one of the rare things that you carry with you for your entire life it is interesting to know the 'average daily cost' of a tattoo.

If your tattoo costs $200, you get the tattoo when you are in your twenties or thirties and say you live until you are 70 years old. The average daily cost of your tattoo is only .01 to . 013 cents a day. or .03-.04 cents a month.

42

Tipping is up to you as the client. If you are pleased with the service that was offered, and happy with the results, tips are always appreciated by your artist. A tip is something the artist gets to keep outright as opposed to the actual amount you pay for your tattoo which goes to pay many other expenses before a portion of it is paid to the artist. It lets your artist know you were happy with them, the experience and the final outcome of the tattoo.

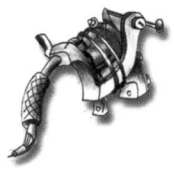

Your Artist and Their Time

Most tattoo artists do not enjoy bartering over the price of their services. I am not sure why people feel that tattoos are worthy of the barter system but they are not. Does a person go to Walmart and try to barter with the cashier "Hey I know you want $50 for this lamp but I will give you $40 cash!" or to their local diner and ask "Me and my friend are both getting the same meal at the same time can we get a two for one deal?". Tattooing is not in the same field as bartering for your souvenirs in Mexico, your artist does not inflate their prices to account for you wanting to barter for your tattoo.

A tattoo artist is supplying a personal service, like for example a hairdresser or message therapist provides. People who offer personal services only get paid for the time they are working on a client and they can only work on one client at a time. In the case of a hairdresser for example: it is not very often you hear of someone going to their hairdresser and asking for a deal on their hair cut. Think about how many times you have gone to the hairdresser to have your hair done. More times than you will ever have go to a tattoo artist to have the same tattoo redone again, a well done tattoo lasts way longer than a hair cut it does not have to be redone every month or two months often it does not require touch ups for years.

Respect your artists skill and time. Most artist put way more time into creating your beautiful piece of art for you than just the time they spend tattooing you. The larger your tattoo the more time the artist will spend preparing it, that you are not directly paying for. So trying to 'jew' them down in price can be insulting. Another thing to keep in mind is that your tattoo is FOREVER, it is going to last way longer than the take-out you had for lunch, the hair cut you just got or the new lamp you just bought.

There are many things that factor into the cost of a tattoo in a professional shop, not only the supplies used for the actual tattoo, there is overhead that has to be paid in order for the shop to stay open. Overhead is how much it costs to keep the shop open and offer you a good service so you have the best experience possible. Overhead includes everything from the rent and utilities to phone and internet services, insurance, licensing fees, office supplies, art supplies, cleaning supplies and even the toilet tissue and hand towels you and your friends use when you are there and of course the government always wants their cut of the profits. On top of this the artist must pay for the equipment they use to tattoo you such as tattoo machines and power supplies and all the disposables that they use during each tattoo like needles, ink, paper towels, gloves, disinfectant and even the rinse cups they use to rinse the tattoo needles in , etc. Then there is the time they spend designing, drawing and perfecting your tattoo design getting it ready for you, which many artists do not charge extra for. All this has to be paid for from the cost of the tattoo before the artist gets paid for the time they put in physically doing your tattoo. If your artist is not the owner of the shop a percentage of the amount you pay for your tattoo goes to the shop first and each artist will also have personal overhead and supplies they have to pay for as well, before they start making money on the time they spend tattooing. So after expenses the artists themselves receive or are 'payed' a very small amount from what you are paying for your tattoo.

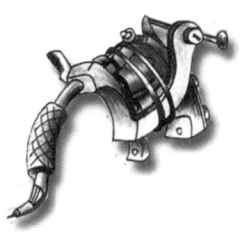

Chapter 7

What To Expect The Day Of Your Tattoo:

Your tattoo is tomorrow what you need to know.

Everyone gets nervous when they are about to get a new tattoo, because it hurts right?! This is especially true when it is your first tattoo you, don't know what to expect and everyone is telling you how terrible it is going to feel. It's like a right of passage to try to scare the bejesus out of people if you already have a tattoo and it is their first one. In reality yes tattoos hurt however in the 14 years I have been tattooing, and I have tattooed over 6500 tattoos on people, in all of that time I have only had one person quit before they were done. Yes, that's right only one. Nine times out of ten after we start my clients say 'That's it? That's not what I expected at all. I can do this.' Try not to over think it and work your self up this only makes it harder to handle your tattoo when you get it done and I have had clients that make themselves sick with worry over it. I always ask my clients if they have ever stubbed their toe, and let them know that stubbing your toe hurts worse than getting a tattoo. I also tell my clients if child birth is a 10 then the average pain level of a tattoo is only a 2 or 3. There are a lot of things you have and will experience in your life that are a lot more painful than a tattoo. Remember the needle barely goes into the skin it is more like a scrape than a needle and nothing like when you go to the doctor.

In any case your job when you're getting a tattoo is to relax, breath and sit as still as you can. This is going to make your tattoo go as smoothly and quickly as possible. Do not move away suddenly while the artist is tattooing, if the needle is still against the skin the artist may not be able to lift it in time and you could rune your tattoo, ending up with messy lines and lines where they do not belong. If you are moving a lot it is really hard even impossible for your artist to make smooth perfect lines for you and your tattoo will end up not looking the way you want it. Jumping around, trying to move away from the tattoo artist as the artist is tattooing and making a lot of noise is only making your tattoo take longer, and making it harder for your tattoo artist to tattoo you. Your tattoo artist is not going to find your antics funny, in a lot of cases all it is going to do is annoy them, and seriously do you really want an annoyed tattoo artist tattooing you?

If you have any medical conditions that you think my affect your getting a tattoo, speak with your tattoo artist about it and they will let you know if you should ask your doctor before getting a tattoo. If you are prone to passing out easily or have seizures let your artist know so they can keep a more careful eye on you while they tattoo.

If you do have a communicable disease such as HIV or Hepatitis, there are many artists that will not tattoo you however there are a few that will, they will take extra precautions when tattooing you. I would hope that you will not go into a shop and lie to an artist about having a communicable disease as the artist has the right to know and decline tattooing anyone with a communicable disease if they are not comfortable.

Get a good nights sleep the night before, try not to go in for your tattoo after a long night of being awake, your tattoo experience will be more pleasant if you do not go in tired or even worse hung over from drinking the night before. Make sure to have a shower and wear clean cloths, the cleaner your skin the better, as your skin is going to be traumatized during the tattoo process. Although your artist will clean your skin thoroughly the cleaner your skin is to start with, the less chance of anything being accidentally introduced into the wound on your skin that could compromise the healing process.

Eat before your tattoo. Eating will stabilize your blood sugars and help your body deal with the trauma better. When you have low blood sugar your body is less able to cope with the endorphins (natural pain killers) and the rise in adrenaline in response to the tattoo process and you could feel light headed, cold and sweaty, dizzy and have upset stomach. Many artists suggest having a donuts before your tattoo as the sugar helps bring up your blood sugar and the dough of the doughnut will help absorb any acid that may be produced in your stomach so you don't feel ill. Bring along some sweet snacks and drinks as this can help if you do happen to feel light headed or ill during the tattoo process, especially when your tattoo is going to take longer than a couple of hours.

You may want to bring someone for moral support, check with your artist to see if family and friends are allowed into the tattoo area with you. Some artists do not allow anyone in the tattoo room but yourself. Bringing a large group of friends can be disruptive to the artist who wants to give you the best possible tattoo. When a group of family and friends is present during the process it can cause the tattoo client to move around more while talking and laughing with their support group which makes the tattoo more difficult for the artist to do. If family and friends are allowed ask them to be respectful of the artist and not to be too rowdy as your artist may ask them to leave if they are too disruptive.

If you have young children find someone to leave your children with, no matter how well behaved your children are. Your tattoo will most likely take longer than they would like and we all know what it is like waiting for someone, and as a child it is especially hard to wait. They can become restless and want to come and be with you, and if they are allowed in the tattoo room with you they may want to sit with you or climb on you. In the process causing your body to move and making it impossible for your artist to do a good job on your tattoo. Many shops do not allow children in the tattoo area at all. There are also shops that do not allow anyone under the age of 18 into the shop.

Wear appropriate clothing. If you are getting a tattoo on your back or shoulders bringing a sweater or jacket that can be put on backwards for the tattoo, thus covering your front and opening up your back to be tattooed. If it is on your legs wear loose sweats or bring shorts to change into for the tattoo. You want to be as comfortable as possible for your tattoo. Don't wear white or your favorite clothes! Ink does tend to travel and it is very easy for your clothes to be stained by the ink. Take it from a tattoo artist, tattoo ink does not wash out of your clothes.

If you have hair long enough to get in the way of the place your tattoo is being done have something to put it up with so it stays out of the way.

There is always the possibility that the extra endorphins and adrenaline that your body is producing to help with the pain of the tattoo can make you feel light headed and dizzy. Let your artist know immediately if this happens. They are trained and prepared to be able to help you through this too. Don't worry it is normal it happens to lots people, occasionally to people that have dozens of tattoos, even when they think the tattoo does not hurt bad at all. When it passes, and it will pass, you will be fine for the rest of the tattoo. This is also why it is a good idea to eat before your tattoo as eating balances your blood sugars and helps you to deal with all the added chemicals your body is producing during the tattoo process.

If at anytime you are not comfortable with something

that your artist is doing or how your tattoo is looking do not be afraid to say something. If your artist is unwilling to work with you do not be afraid to stop the tattoo session and leave. Remember it is your body and your tattoo, you have to be happy with the final result so if at any time during the process something is bothering you speak up. Even if it results in you having to pay for an unfinished tattoo, it is better to have an unfinished tattoo because in the end it will cost less to have it finished by another artist as opposed to you not saying anything and having a finished tattoo you are unhappy with. It will cost you more as a result to have it fixed or covered up. Also speaking up and having your artist work with you to rectify what is bothering you will result in a better tattoo for you. In many cases not speaking up and being unhappy and leaving and telling all your friends and family how unhappy you are when you did nothing to try solve the problem with your artist is unfair to your artist who more often than not could have addressed and rectified your concerns while you were getting tattooed.

If you have discussed your concerns with your artist and are not happy with the results or you just are not comfortable going back to the artist who started your work, for whatever reason you feel you need to go elsewhere to have your tattoo finished or fixed, there are artists who will do this for you. There are some artists who refuse to finish or touch another artists work. Do not be discouraged as there are also artists who will.

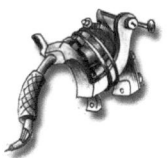

How long will Your Tattoo take?

There are many factors that will determine the length of time it will take to get your tattoo. Reality TV has done a lot to help boost the popularity of tattoos, however the 'magic' of television editing has placed unrealistic time factors and expectations on getting a tattoo.

Expect a small tattoo around 3" x 3" to take anywhere from 45 minutes to 1 1/2 hours to complete depending on the detail and color of your tattoo, what part of the body you get it done on, how many breaks you have to take and the experience of the artist. The more detailed and colorful your tattoo the longer it will take to complete. So even for the smallest tattoo expect to be in the shop for at least an hour.

Larger pieces like back pieces and sleeves will take several sittings of several hours each to complete.

Getting a tattoo on fresh skin is going to take less time than getting a cover up tattoo, which can take two or three times longer to complete and in some cases more than one session. If your getting your tattoo in an awkward spot that is hard for your tattoo artist to access easily this too will add extra time on to how long it will take to complete your tattoo.

Remember tattoo artists are working with your 'living' canvas and the condition and type of skin in the location of your tattoo on your body are major factors in how long it will take to get your tattoo. As previously mentioned some skin types are easier to tattoo and thus the tattoo process will go quicker, other areas are harder to tattoo and as a result it will take longer to do your tattoo.

How well you can sit is another factor, if you can sit still for longer periods of time without taking breaks your tattoo will take less time to do as opposed to someone who needs to take a lot of breaks and moves around a lot, as every time a tattoo client moves the artist has to stop tattooing thus extending the amount of time it takes to do your tattoo.

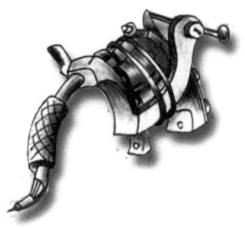

Chapter 8

Looking After Your Fresh Tattoo

Tattoos are an open wound. The larger the tattoo the larger the open wound. The most crucial time in tattoo healing is the first 3 to 4 days. It is during this time that your body is working to 'seal' your wound, so nothing will get in and cause an infection. Your tattoo will be tender and slightly red around the edges for the first few days. During this time your tattoo will look fresh and often shiny from the plasma your body is producing to keep contaminants that your tattoo may come in contact with from causing an infection. The top layer of your skin, the Keratin which acts as a waterproof barrier for your skin, has been compromised. When you get a tattoo the tattoo needles have to go through this top layer of skin thus damaging it so that your skins ability to keep moisture and contaminates out is compromised. Thus the skin in the area of your tattoo is more like a sponge and can absorb extra water which will cause extra scabbing on your tattoo. This is why it is imperative to not 'soak' your fresh tattoo in water such as bathtubs, swimming pools, hot tubs, oceans, sinks, even in that extra long shower, because your skin will absorb water. Your body could also be unable to block contaminates from dirty water entering into the tattoo from places like swimming pools and hot tubs, until the top layer of skin has a chance to regenerate and become water repellent once again. The time it takes for this to happen varies from person to person depending on the location on your body, size and coverage of the tattoo, and could take anywhere from 5 days to sometimes as long as 30 days if your tattoo is heavily scabbed.

As your body heals in the first few days of healing, the traumatized top layer of skin on your tattoo will form into a thin dry layer to protect the damaged skin underneath. This will be the layer of skin that peals off once a new layer has been formed under it. Be aware that some color will come off with this layer of skin when it peals off as the tattoo ink is in this layer as well as the layer of skin that the ink will stay in permanently. This may slightly affect the final color of your tattoo, think of your tattoo when healed as being under a layer of tinted glass, the tint level on the skin will effect the brightness of the tattoo when it is finished healing. The darker the skin the less bright the colors of your tattoo will look.

The location of the tattoo also will factor into how long and how well it heals. If your tattoo is in an area where movement of your body is causing your skin to constantly stretch this will irritate the tattoo and it will take longer to heal. If your tattoo is in an area where there is constant movement of the skin, your body also will continually send plasma to protect this area of your tattoo from getting an infection, keeping it wet and causing it to take longer for the top layer of skin to dry out and seal. When this happens and the plasma is continually having to come to the surface of your tattoo you will also find that you have more scabbing due to the build up of dried plasma on the top of your tattoo. The thicker the scabbing the more painful your tattoo will be during the healing process. As a result of thick scabbing it will take longer for new skin to regenerate underneath the scabbing and longer for the scabbing to be released from the newly formed skin. Picking at scabbing before it is ready to come off will remove color from your tattoo because the scabbing is still bonded to the lower layers of skin where your tattoo will remain and your tattoo color is located. If the scabbing is left to heal on its own eventually a new layer of keratin skin will form underneath the scab and your body will naturally allow the scab to dry out and it will fall off on its own leaving the tattoo color unaffected. Occasionally the scab is in a location that can be rubbed off accidentally and will take some color from your tattoo with it. If you do lose spots of color because of a scab coming off before it is ready it is easy for your tattoo artist to tattoo over these areas again once your tattoo is fully healed to replace the missing color.

If your body is already trying to heal from something, be it a common cold, child birth or even surgery it will take longer and be more difficult for your body to heal your tattoo. Complications often occur in these instances such as irritation, inconstant healing, excessive scabbing and even infections because your body does not have enough resources to dedicated to the healing of your tattoo.

Scabbing can also happen when a tattoo artist accidentally over works your skin traumatizing it to a deeper layer. The more traumatized your skin the more plasma your body will produce to prevent contaminants from entering the wound and as a result the longer it takes for your tattoo to dry and seal. The result is heavier scabbing, this can happen over just small areas of your tattoo or over the whole tattoo.

Ideally a tattoo will only be moist for the first 24 hours, after this time the wound will begin to dry out and seal itself over the next three days, the end result being a thin layer of dry looking skin over the whole tattoo, that will in the next 3 - 7 days peel off like a sun burn. Small areas of scabbing can take longer to heal, this is not unusual, left to heal naturally your tattoo will not be adversely affected.

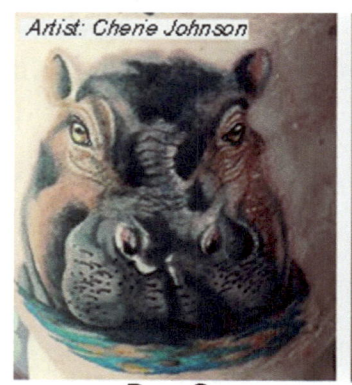 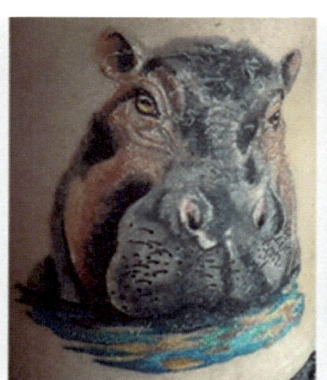 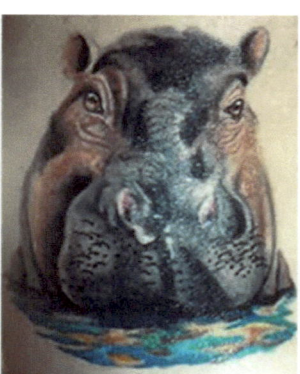

Day One
Immediately after
bandage removal

Day Four
Peeling

Day Seven
Done Peeling

As you can see from the above photos, on day one there is a slight redness and swelling around the edge of the tattoo, by day four the tattoo is peeling like a sunburn and on day seven the tattoo is finished with it's first peel. At this point the tattoo still looks slightly shiny and this will be the case until it is totally healed which could take about one month.

If your tattoo is taking longer to heal watch for warning signs. If after 4 or 5 days your tattoo is still very red around the edges, swollen and generally sore to the touch or if your tattoo develops these symptoms during the healing process it is a good idea start using an antibiotic cream on your tattoo. Often the swelling, redness and soreness of your tattoo could be a result of the area it is in. Again where your skin is always moving or being irritated by brushing up against things can be red and sore looking longer than areas that are covered and don't move a lot. Images of tattoos that are healing badly are readily available for viewing on the internet. If your concerned ask your tattoo artist if what you are experiencing is normal for the area.

If your tattoo still continues to be red, swollen and sore or develops extra symptoms like puss and/or red spider veins, these are signs of infection, the spider veins coming from the edges of your tattoo can also be indicative of blood poisoning. Something has been introduced into the tattoo during the healing process and may have caused an infection. Go to the doctor you may need antibiotics to help heal your tattoo.

As mentioned before allergic reactions to tattoo pigments do occasionally occur. If you find there are certain areas of your tattoo that are swollen, feel hard and are itchy and the top laying of skin is very dry and is constantly peeling, long after your tattoo should be or is healed, this is most likely your body trying to get rid of a pigment it is allergic too for some reason. You can purchase topical cortisone creams in the pharmacy and use them on your tattoo. If after a few weeks the itching and swelling has not abated you can get a stronger cortisone cream from the doctor. The more intense the reaction is the longer it will take to settle down however it will settle down over time. If you just have a mild reaction where you find certain areas on your tattoo are very itchy off and on but is not severely swollen or not swollen at all, again you can use a topical over the counter cortisone cream whenever it is itchy and over time your body will settle down and the itching will go away. Sometimes this can take several months to go away.

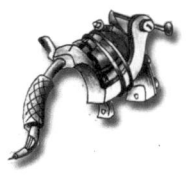

General Tattoo After Care Instructions

There are many different aftercare instructions given to clients. This aftercare guide is the most thorough guide we could give you. This information is for your personal benefit and may be used, modified, or discarded accordingly to your specific needs. These aftercare suggestions are guidelines, not a prescribed course of care. You must be responsible for your actions there is no 100% positive way to avoid trouble during your healing, sometimes things happen beyond anyones control. You are responsible for your own tattoo aftercare. Tattooing causes trauma to the skin, your skin has been poked with needles. You are healing an injury, treat your tattoo as such.

Keep in mind that healing time and amount of trauma recovery vary greatly and depends on many things. Each person's skin type and immune system, the tattoo you received, the artist who did the tattoo procedure, equipment and inks used, and of course the degree of aftercare. What works for someone else, may not work for you. Always use common sense and good hygiene and you'll be fine.

Depending on the bandage applied some artists may instruct you leave it on from 3 hours to as long as 24 hours.

After removing the bandage wash away blood and plasma thoroughly using mild soap and water. You may have to soap up and wash your tattoo twice the first time you wash it after removing bandage. We recommend you dry your tattoo using clean lint free paper towel as there is no bacteria on it, you never know who used a towel or face cloth before you and what they may have wiped.

After removing the bandage and washing your tattoo it is important to:

Keep your tattoo clean and dry

Do not keep covered beyond the first day unless you need to cover it to keep clean for work in this case cover with a clean **NON-STICK** bandaid pad. Remove the bandaid pad and wash your tattoo after each work day.

Washing your tattoo will kill bacteria collected throughout the day and lightly moisturize your scabs. This is the most important part of your aftercare, more important than applying ointment. You can skip the ointment, but never skip the washing.

Always wash your hands before washing, handling orṏ applying ointment or lotion to your tattoo!

Wash your tattoo 2 - 3 times a day (morning, afternoon, night) for 7 - 9 days longer if you have scabs then continue this regime until the scabs fall off. After this you may return to washing your tattoo once a day, but still be gentle. Wash your tattoo with a unscented antibacterial hand soap. Always wash your hands thoroughly with antibacterial hand soap first before touching your tattoo.

DO NOT use wash cloths, loofas or scrubbers of any kind. Gently lather antibacterial hand soap onto your hands and rub over your tattoo with your fingertips. Rinse thoroughly. Pat dry with a clean lint free towel or quality paper towel Bountie is a good choice. Don't be cheap with the paper towels, it's worth the extra few dollars to get the good ones as the cheap towel will fall apart and leave paper fibers on your tattoo. Allow a minimum of 30 minutes to air dry.

Keep your hands off your tattoo, unless you are washing your tattoo or applying moisturizer, there is no other reason for your hands to come in contact with your tattoo while it is healing.

You can shower but use the 'last wet first dry' rule, do not take long showers be quick as cleaning your tattoo is always good however soaking your tattoo for extended periods of time is not good for it.

For the first 3 or 4 days allow your tattoo to air dry for 30 minutes to an hour or longer after washing it before applying any product or covering it with your clothing. Plasma oozing is normal it will make your tattoo look sweaty or moist, it is your body's natural defence against infection. Oozing usually occurs within the first 24 hours of initial tattooing, however in some instances it can continue longer. Make sure your tattoo is dry before dressing or going to bed. If you find your clothing or bedding have dried and stuck to your tattoo, try not to pull them of dry. Wet the cloth that is stuck to you with clean water to loosen the dried plasma and gently remove it from tattoo. During the first few days of healing the tattoo may seep ink, blood or plasma which could stain clothing, sheets or other fabrics.

Keep your tattoo moisturized, however do not keep it 'wet' with your product, as a tattoo that is too wet will develop larger scabs and take longer to heal. There are specialty tattoo healing products on the market you can use, also skin moisturizers work as well be sure it is unscented, lanolin & Vaseline free, in other words not greasy. Apply a very SMALL amount of moisturizer once or twice a day for the first 2 to 3 days. Spread a very small amount of moisturizer with clean fingertips thinly over tattoo you should not see any product sitting on top of the skin when your done, if there is extra product visible wipe it off. After 3 to 4 days moisturize whenever your tattoo looks dry or is itchy for remainder of the aftercare regime.

Once your scabs have flaked off, your ink is "sealed in". Your skin is not finished healing though. You may notice lots dry and flaky skin coming off of your tattoo. Your skin will appear cloudy at first, making your tattoo seem dull. This is due to the skins cells still healing to their normal condition. Liberally apply fragrance and dye free moisturizing lotion for the next month or so.

Make sure your sheets and bedding are clean the first week of aftercare. You don't want to get an infection because your tattoo has come into contact with something on your sheets during the night. Also make sure clothing touching your tattoo during the day are clean.

Stay away from these products during the healing process:\|

Vaseline
A & D ointment\|
Neosporin or any triple antibiotic ointments\|
Fruit scented hand soaps\|
Lotions that contain "alcohol"

Beware of your Pets

Pets bring many potential dangers to tattoo aftercare. Hair, dander, drool, urine and feces are all present and very real dangers in your home environment while healing any injury. Things can get bad very fast, infections are real. Be aware of your surroundings. Clean and disinfect all areas you may come in contact with that your pet also has access too. Do not allow your fresh tattoo to come into contact with your pet for at least 1 week after getting tattooed.

You can use ice to help reduce swelling, soreness and over all discomfort of your tattoo just wrap your tattoo with clean saran wrap and place your ice pack over the protective film. When you are done remove the film and wash your tattoo.

Wear soft, comfortable clothing. There is nothing worse

than going through your work day wearing jeans that are constantly irritating your tattoo. This causes unnecessary irritation and will prolong your healing time, and could possibly cause permanent damage to your tattoo.

A healthy diet and drinking plenty of water will help heal your tattoo which is now a part of your skin. Proper nutrition and hydration are key to recovering quickly and with less chances of something going wrong. If your immune system is weak it will be harder to heal your tattoo.If you workout try to wait at least a few days after your tattoo before you hit the gym. If you have to work out it is best to not workout a full routine for at least 2 weeks after getting tattooed. Do half your normal routine for half the time for the two weeks following a tattoo. Always wash your tattoo immediately before and immediately after your working out.

Protect your tattoo from sunlight especially during the first two weeks after your tattoo. Your skin is traumatized and could burn very easily. Do not apply sun screen until it is fully healed. After you get tattooed and it has healed treat the tattooed area like baby skin as it will take up to six months for your body to regenerate the skin back to its original condition before it was tattooed.

DO NOT pick, scratch, or peel any loose skin or scabs, they will come off when they are ready.

Absolutely NO SWIMMING OR HOT TUBBING UNTIL THE TATTOO IS COMPLETELY HEALED with no pealing or scabbing left on the tattoo. A fresh tattoo is a perfect place for bacteria from such activities to breed and cause serious infections. Short showers only until completely healed (approximately 2 weeks)

NO direct sunlight or tanning beds until completely healed. Constant unprotected exposure to sunlight while your tattoo is healing could cause sunburn and/or fade your tattoo.

DO NOT shave over your tattoo until it has healed.

DO NOT put make-up or perfume on your tattoo until it is fully healed.

Do not scratch if itchy during the healing process

Average healing time is from 5 to 10 days. Everyone heals differently, some take longer than others. Do not panic if it is longer

If your tattoo is red, swollen and sore to the touch for longer than 4 or 5 days you may need to see your doctor.

If you are in any way concerned about your tattoos healing progress contact your tattoo artist

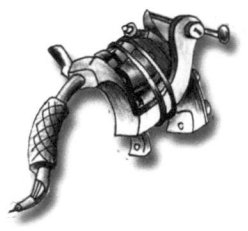

Touch ups

Do not panic if you need a touch up. If the tattoo heals and it does not look like what you expected, it can have a second session to get it to where you want it to be.

Remember:
Your tattoo artist is a human,
they are not machines.

There are many variables that could require you need a touch up such as :

*How much your skin swells during the tattoo process can affect how even your lines are and how solid your color is.

*If you are slightly ill at the time of your tattoo can make it harder for the artist to work with your skin.

*Some medications and even Marijuana contain chemicals that when used can make it harder to get the ink to go into your skin and stay there and can require two or more sessions to make the tattoo look smooth and solid.

*Alcohol use can cause a tattoo to bleed even days after you have been tattooed affecting the final look of your tattoo when healed.

*All areas of your body tattoo and heal, differently. Some skin types are more delicate and take longer to heal such as the inside of your arm others, such as your neck, hands, wrists and feet for example, are harder to work with and more often than not require two sessions to make a tattoo look really good.

*The type of tattoo you get is also a factor, lettering for example: the finer and smaller the writing the less likely it will be perfectly even when it heals and will need some tightening up. Also the more solid a color is the more likely it could heal with lighter patches of color. Colored outlines can also heal inconstantly.

*The time of year, how much sun exposure you allowed onto your tattoo.

*How well you looked after your tattoo during the healing process.

*Rough and tight clothing rubbing on your tattoo can cause color loss.

It is not uncommon to need touch ups to tighten up a tattoo once it is all healed. In the end every skin type and every person will heal differently.

The best time to get a touch up is approximately 6 weeks after you get your tattoo. This gives your tattoo plenty of time to heal. If you have any concerns stop in and see your artist about it.

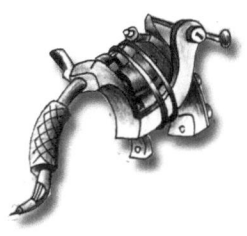

Chapter 9

Cover Ups

Everyone makes mistakes and a lot of us have tattoos we regret. That tattoo that sounded like a great idea while you were at that party and your buddy just happened to have that new tattoo 'gun' that just arrived from eBay. Could be it was the drunken dare tattoo or perhaps it was the tattoo you tried to do on yourself. Maybe it was done in a shop but did not turn out the way you wanted. Of course there is always those that fell in love got that name that they swore would be forever and it turned out not to be so permanent and now you do not want to look at it anymore. Maybe you just outgrew your tattoo, it is not relevant anymore or it is very old and faded. Whatever the reason cover up tattoos have become very popular and some artists are becoming very good at knowing how to cover up almost any tattoo to make it more appealing to you.

If you happen to have a tattoos you want covered up be sure to find an artist that has been doing this type of tattooing for a while. It takes special planning and knowledge to design a new tattoo to completely cover and hide an old tattoo. You will also be a lot more limited in exactly what your tattoo can be when it is covering an existing tattoo as not all tattoo designs will completely cover and hide an old tattoo, and as a result when it is finished you will still see the old tattoo underneath of it. If your artist is not experienced in cover up work they may not realize this and you could end up with your old tattoo still very visible under your new tattoo.

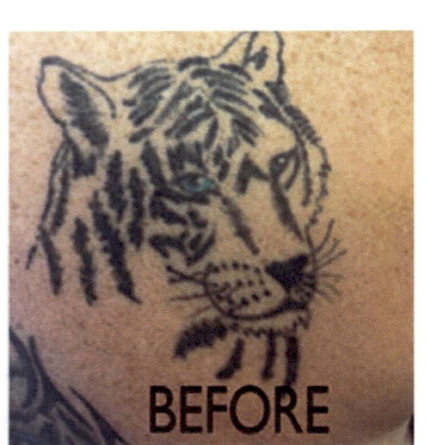

BEFORE

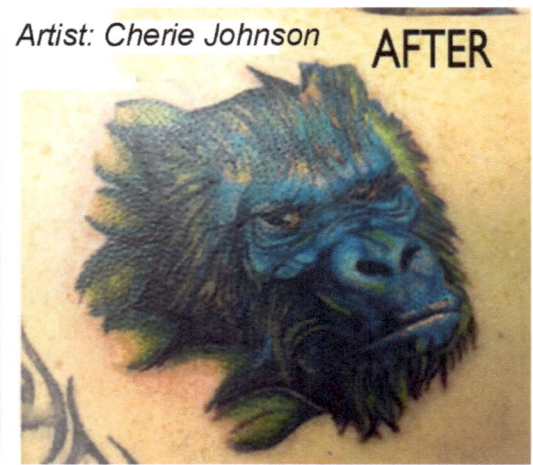

Artist: Cherie Johnson

AFTER

You are not necessarily limited to a black tattoo to cover up an existing tattoo, a tattoo artist experienced in doing cover up work will be able to design a cover up utilizing the existing lines, color and free space in the tattoo you want covered up to create a beautiful new tattoo over top.

Be prepared for the cover tattoo to be quite a bit larger than the tattoo you are covering up and to be more expensive than a tattoo done on fresh skin. Also the more complicated a cover up tattoo is the longer it is going to take, often quite a bit longer to get done than a tattoo done on fresh skin. It may also require two or more sessions to ensure that it is covering up the tattoo underneath well.

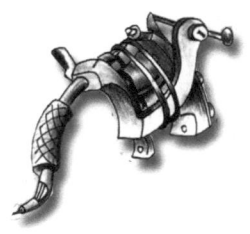

Chapter 10

Thinking of Getting
Tattooed In a House
What You Need To Know

Perhaps you are considering getting at tattoo from an artist out of their home. Although you may occasionally come across a really good tattoo artist working out of their home there are a few things you should consider and keep in mind before you decide to go to someones home for a tattoo.

In a professional shop tattoo artists are regulated by the health board they have to follow certain guidelines on cleanliness, also products used must be properly packaged and sterilized such as needles, tubes and inks. Tattoo shops have to carry insurance as well.

In someones home, unless they have a dedicated space that is specifically for tattooing which in some cases could be health board approved, you have to be extra cautious. Health board approved locations require the tattoo area to have 100% cleanable surfaces and have access to a dedicated sink with hot and cold running water in the room used only for the tattoo area, so not a shared bathroom or kitchen sink.

Are you being tattooed in a kitchen or family room?

These are communal general use rooms that are very hard to keep totally disinfected and free of things that could transfer into and contaminate your tattoo causing infection. Especially if there are pets and children in the home.

Are all the surfaces able to be cleaned properly and disinfected?

Cloth chairs and carpeting can not be properly cleaned so it creates an environment with allergens and microbes that could easily transfer into your fresh tattoo.

Are there pets allowed in the space, before or during the tattoo, spreading dirt and fur that could accidentally get introduced into your tattoo during the tattooing process?

Pets are very dirty, they roll around on the ground that is covered in dirt and germs picking it up in their fur and bringing it along with them wherever they go. They can also get feces and urine on their fur and bring that into these common areas to be left behind and it could be transferred into your tattoo.

Are all the products being used on you for the tattoo new and properly sterilized, including the needles, tubes and tattoo ink?

It is possible to get an illness from unsterilized

equipment. Especially if anything that is being used was previously used on another person.

Is the artist schooled in the dangers of cross contamination and blood born pathogens?

Is your artist aware of the dangers of cross contamination and blood born pathogens or diseases that can be transferred by way of blood from one person to another. There are certain precautions that each artist must take to prevent this from happening to you.

If your concerned does the artist have insurance just for the tattoo process?

Many insurance companies will not insure a tattoo artist working out of there own home.

Getting a tattoo at a party from a friend while you are laying on the cloth sofa that the cat just rolled on or your buddies just spilled their drinks on, is probably not the cleanest place to get tattooed and could result in something transferring in your tattoo and the tattoo becoming infected.

Another thing you might want to keep in mind is the quality of tattoo you are going to receive, how experienced is the artist that is going to tattoo you?

Tattooing may look easy but anyone who has done it will tell you it is not as easy as it looks. It takes a long time sometimes years of practice to get consistent and really good at tattooing. It really is not as easy as picking up a pencil and drawing a picture on a piece of paper. For one thing there is no eraser on the end of a tattoo machine and once the ink has been transferred into your skin there is no going back.

If you are aware of the quality of tattoo you may get from an artist just learning and are willing to take the risk to help them out on their learning journey that's great!

However if you are expecting and wanting a professional quality tattoo, going to someone who is just starting out because they may be cheaper may not be the wisest choice to make.

Enjoy your next new tattoo!